Elena's Ride

by Susan Blackaby
illustrated by
Meryl Treatner

MODERN CURRICULUM PRESS
Pearson Learning Group

The sun was just edging over the tops of the trees as Elena made her bed. She straightened the pillows. She pulled the faded patchwork quilt into place, patting it smooth. Out her window, she could see her cousin and uncle. They walked across the courtyard, heading out toward the corral. Tío Diego, her uncle, waved his coffee mug in the air as he talked to Pepe. One of the dogs danced along between them. Already the sky was washed with a glimmer of clear, golden light.

Elena wondered what her mom was doing at that exact moment. Maybe she was still sleeping after a long night of studying. Maybe she was braiding her hair and planning her day. Maybe she had gotten up early too, and was packing her books and papers into Elena's old book bag. Maybe she was walking across campus to class.

Somewhere in the house, a clock chimed.
It measured the hours in somber, even tones.
Elena pulled her hair into a ponytail. Then
she sat at her desk. She took out a piece of
paper. She used colored pencils to make a
sketch of the view from her window.
Below it she wrote
a note.

Dear Mama,
    It is daybreak, and I am wide
awake. I have been on the ranch
only two weeks and already
I can't sleep past 5:30. Pinch
me! This can't be real! I
miss you.

    I love you,
    E.

It had taken a few weeks for Elena to feel settled on her uncle's Texas ranch. For one thing, she missed her mom and dad. She had made a deal to stay for the summer. Her mom needed to go to school full time. Her dad was starting his new job as a pilot. But it wasn't easy to be away from them. For another, she was used to the color, variety, and noise of the city. Something new and unexpected was around every corner. On the ranch, there were no corners. The land stretched out to the horizon. It was broken only by the silver streak of the creek. To the west, the rugged mountains rose up sharply to meet the sky. The faint outline of the nearest town disappeared in the hazy glimmer of the highway. The city was a journey away.

On the ranch, one day seemed to fall into step behind the next. Elena worked with her cousin, Pepe. He patiently carried out repeated routines. Every job followed a set number of steps and movements. They were done in the same order and in the same way every time. Elena began to understand the slow, steady rhythm of saddling a horse, curling up rope, and unlatching and swinging open a gate.

Elena helped out with early morning chores. Once the animals were cared for and the rest of her jobs were finished, Elena was free to take her sketch pad and wander. She liked to go along the creek or up the canyons that led into the mountains. She always took one of the dogs with her, along with water and a snake-bite kit. She was learning about the earth and sky. Her parents, her grandparents, and even her great-grandparents had called this place home.

In the evenings, the family stayed at the dining room table long after the meal was cleared away. Pepe played with the wax that dripped down the big candles. The light flickered. Tío Diego told Elena stories about growing up on the ranch with her father and aunts.

Elena studied the portraits of her grandparents. The photos hung on the dining room wall. She had her grandmother's slim fingers and her grandfather's long, straight nose. Their dark eyes seemed to fill with laughter and life as Tío Diego talked about the family.

If only Elena could get used to the horses that Tío Diego raised. They were huge and powerful. Elena tried to be open-minded about learning to ride, but she was frightened. And she was sure the horses could sense it. Pepe teased her about being a chicken. She did not care. Riding made her stomach flip. Once she was up on the horse, the only thing that she could think about was how to get down. Tío Diego gave her jobs to do in the horse barn. They were supposed to help make her feel more at ease around horses, but they only magnified her fear. Tío Diego tried to find time for Elena to ride every day. She did not disobey his wishes, but she was happy when he was too busy to remember her lesson.

Elena sealed the envelope. Her bare feet slid over the cool, slick tile and slapped down the stairs to the main hall. In the kitchen, her Aunt Marta and Anna, the cook, greeted her.

"Ah, it is our sleepyhead," said Anna with a wink.

Tía Marta gave Elena a hug. "What is this?" Marta plucked the letter from Elena's hand. "Another letter!"

"Oh, I just write short letters," said Elena.

"Yes," said Anna. "Our Elena has only three things to say. I hate horses, I hate horses, and I hate horses. Is that right?"

Elena laughed. "I never said I hated horses! In fact, from far away, they are beautiful. Up close they are kind of big, but from far away, they are just right. I send Mama pictures too." Elena picked up a pen and made a quick sketch on a napkin. It showed a horse grazing by the creek. "See? Like that."

"That is a very tiny horse, Elena," said Tía Marta, looking closely at the drawing. "Hardly a steed! It's no bigger than a cricket. Nothing to be frightened of."

"Well, that's the way I like them," said Elena, accepting a mug of cocoa and a hot roll from Anna.

Tía Marta turned back to her work. "This land, these horses, they are in your blood, Elena. Sooner or later you will like to ride."

Elena gathered her supplies and went outside. A cool breeze stirred the shade under the porch. One of the dogs lifted its head as Elena passed by. It hopped up to follow. After a few steps it sat and waited, as if it needed permission to come along.

"Come along, Tip, unless you would rather stay here with these lazy old guys," said Elena.

Tío Diego waved as Elena and Tip passed by the corral. He was watching Pepe work with a colt. The colt was kicking up smoky puffs of dust.

Elena and Tip crossed the creek and a broad expanse of land before starting up a narrow trail. The trail followed a stand of pine trees that grew in a seam between the rocks. The rise was gentle. Elena could hardly tell that they were going up until she stopped to look back down the valley. The ranch buildings looked like little islands in a sandy sea.

The trail followed the tree line a little farther and then rose up, rocky and steep. Tip's feet skittered on the loose gravel. Elena was about to turn back when the trail suddenly leveled off onto a huge flat rock. Cliffs rose up on one side, and the valley stretched out below them.

Elena settled herself on a rocky ledge. She shared her water with Tip and then took out her sketch pad. She drew a picture of the rocky crags hanging in space. She wondered if her dad had climbed to this place and dreamed of becoming a pilot.

Dear Daddy,

I am up above the ranch, surrounded by sky. I hope it is cool and clear where you are too.

I miss you.

Love,

E.

Tip barked at the sound of crunching gravel. Elena looked up from her sketch pad to see Pepe on horseback, quickly side-stepping and skidding over the last part of the trail.

"Hey there!" said Pepe.

"Hi!" said Elena, jumping up. "How did you get up here?"

"Oh, it was a little bit tricky in places. But this steed is as sure-footed as a mountain goat."

Pepe leaned down and patted the horse's neck. "Good fella," he said quietly.

Tip's tail wagged. "Yeah, right. You too," laughed Pepe.

Elena looked at the horse's lathered neck and glistening body.

"I still can't believe you made it," she said.

Pepe hopped off his steed and took off the saddle bag. "Steady and fearless too. I am going to call him the Ridge Runner."

"Yeah, well you'd better park him away from the edge, or you can rename him Tumbleweed," said Elena.

"Good point!" said Pepe.

Pepe led the horse to a spot back against the cliff face. Then he pointed to a flat rock and motioned for Elena to join him.

"Anna packed us a picnic," he said. "I spotted you part way up the mountain and figured you might get hungry."

"You could see me from all the way down there?" Elena said.

"I saw your red shirt, silly," said Pepe, setting the food out on the rock. "You were pretty easy to spot until you got up into the trees."

"Well, it isn't as though I was hiding or running away or something."

"Oh, no," said Pepe. "You are only about fifty miles from the nearest riding lesson, that's all!"

"Hmm, well, I am starving," said Elena, reaching for a sandwich.

"Isn't this a cool place?" said Pepe. "If it were spring, a little creek would be running through here. We'd be sitting by a waterfall. I hardly ever come up here when it is dry like this."

Pepe shaded his eyes with his hand and looked up. His gaze rested on the cliff face. He pointed.

"Look up there," he said. "Do you think that is a cave?"

Elena could see a dark shadow in the rocks. It did look like an opening of some kind, but it was up too high to see clearly.

She shrugged. "I don't know. It could just be a nesting spot. Or it could lead to a lost mine."

"Do you think so?" said Pepe, looking surprised.

"Oh sure," said Elena. "Filled with silver and precious stones right up to the brim." She leaned back against a rock and started to make a sketch of Tip and Pepe.

"Well, I am going to investigate," said Pepe.

Before Elena had a chance to object, Pepe was scrambling up the rock face.

"Are you nuts?" she yelled. "What are you doing?"

"I'm just going to see what this is," Pepe called down to her.

"Come down! You're going to fall! Something terrible will happen! Don't do this!" Elena cried.

"I'm fine," called Pepe. "It's like climbing a ladder."

Pepe was lying flat against the rock face, gripping his fingers in a rock seam and feeling for a solid spot to put his foot. He moved like a spider, stretching and bending his way higher and higher. When he got up to the opening, he pulled himself up so that he was squatting, crouched on the narrow ledge.

"You were right!" he yelled. "It is a mine shaft! It looks pretty neat too!"

"Don't you dare go any farther, Pepe," yelled Elena.

"I won't," said Pepe, leaning into the shaft entrance. "I can't see much of anything anyway."

Just then there was a loud crack that echoed off the rock face. Elena was showered with tumbling pebbles. Pepe did not even have a chance to yell before the cave-in. He just disappeared into the darkness.

Elena screamed Pepe's name and then clapped her hands over her mouth. She held her breath and listened for Pepe's voice. Then she heard it, faint and hollow, from deep inside the mountain.

"Elena! Elena! I'm OK! But get help!"

"Are you hurt?" she yelled, cupping her hands around her mouth.

"No. But I'm stuck! Ropes! Bring ropes!"

Elena told Tip to stay put. Then she turned and
ran to the horse. He nodded and stomped at the
ground. She reached for the reins and threw them
over his head. She quickly led him up beside a
boulder so that she could boost herself up to mount.
She got her foot in the stirrup and yanked on the
pommel to pull herself up and swing into the saddle.
Then, without hesitating for a moment, she took the
reins and spun the horse around. She aimed for the
place where the trail wound down through the rocks
and ledges and trees.

The horse leaped forward. He plunged down the steep bank, sending rocks and gravel flying. Elena leaned into each turn, clinging to the horse's neck when he pitched forward, struggling to hang on as he slid. Once they were in the trees, Elena kept her head down. She ducked under low-hanging branches as the horse raced down through a blur of green. In one final leap, they reached the edge of the valley. Then Elena turned the horse toward the ranch.

"Hurry!" whispered Elena, and they flew at full gallop to get help.

Tío Diego had seen Elena coming down the mountain. He met her at the creek. She gasped for air as she told him what had happened.

"Tell Clara and Juan to meet me up on table rock," he said. Then he reached out and squeezed her shoulder.

"Go."

His eyes were somber, his voice was barely a whisper. His horse splashed across the creek and up the bank and Tío Diego was soon lost in a cloud of dust.

Elena rode on to the ranch and sent the two ranch hands back to help. Tía Marta made sure they took plenty of rope with them, and Anna gave them water and a first-aid kit. Then Elena and the women waited, keeping an eye on the tree line.

Elena walked the horse around the corral to cool him off. She inspected his legs to be sure that he had not hurt himself as he dove down the mountain. Then she brushed him and gave him food and water. She was just putting his tack away when she heard Tía Marta call. She hurried into the courtyard. Pepe was getting off Tío Diego's horse. Pepe was dirty and stiff. He gave Elena a sheepish grin. Tip ran up to her, wagging his tail.

"Were you scared?" Pepe asked.

"Yes! You fell head first into the mine! I'll say I was scared!" cried Elena. "I thought my heart was going to jump out of my mouth!"

Pepe had a confused look on his face. "No, not then. I mean when you were riding down the mountain on my horse. Were you scared?"

Everyone waited for Elena to answer.

A smile slowly lit up Elena's face. She had not been scared. During the ride she was fearless. Pepe's horse had carried her safely and swiftly down the mountain, as she knew he would.

"No, I wasn't," said Elena. "After all, horses are in my blood. And that horse is as sure-footed as a mountain goat. Which is more than I can say for some people!"